Perfect
EXMOOR

NEVILLE STANIKK

HALSGROVE

First published in Great Britain in 2008

For more images by the author visit:
www.northdevonpics.co.uk

Title page image: *Heather and a hawthorn bush on Withypool Hill*

British Library Cataloguing-in-Publication Data
A CIP record for this title is available from the British Library

ISBN 978 1 84114 718 5

HALSGROVE
Halsgrove House
Ryelands Industrial Estate
Bagley Road, Wellington,
Somerset TA21 9PZ
Tel: 01823 653777
Fax: 01823 216796
email: sales@halsgrove.com
website: www.halsgrove.com

Printed and bound by Grafiche Flaminia, Italy

INTRODUCTION

This is not an illustrated guide to Exmoor. It's not comprehensive – there are missing views that I simply don't have a good enough picture of. I've been to those places many times but the light hasn't been right and, as far as landscape photography goes, that's what matters.

And getting the perfect light is the final part of the process that us landscape photographers have in common. After that, after we've actually got the picture, our motivations for wanting other people to see the beauty in those images can be very different.

Some of us want people to get fired up about conservation and the environment. Some want them to regret the loss of the countryside and its traditions. Some are patriotic and try to find as many Olde Worlde scenes as they can. Some love the area so much, they want everyone to come and visit. And some, like me, see everything as a setting for a scene from a film.

I suppose I might claim I'm a filmmaker who can't afford actors or costumes or props or even a movie camera but I think I'm more of a location scout because I don't really know what the scene would be about or who'd be in it, just that it would make an ideal backdrop.

But if I am a location scout, I'm a pretty poor one as I'm far too idealistic. I could only be a scout for a film company who could be anywhere within a few seconds as they'd need to make instant use of that patch of mist or that ray of sunlight I'd found. So I think I'll describe myself as a location scout for films that are never going to get made.

Maybe R. D. Blackmore, the author of *Lorna Doone*, saw Exmoor in this way except, in his case, he actually did get something made. In his famous novel, set in 1675, it takes John Ridd, the hero, a whole day and night on horseback to travel a mere twenty miles north from Tiverton across Exmoor to the tiny hamlet of Oare where, nearby, the villains of the piece, the Doone family, can live their outlaw life, virtually unmolested, in the valley of Badgworthy Water.

To me, Exmoor has vast open landscapes that make you understand why that journey would have taken that long, and secret valleys that virtually invite you to populate them with vivid characters especially as there are so few actual people around.

More than that though, Exmoor seems timeless. Blackmore didn't have to make an effort to see Exmoor in the seventeenth century because it isn't anchored in time. There could be cavemen, Romans, knights or lost astronauts. To use a cliché, the possibilities are endless, so although you'll see these pictures however you wish, my intention with each one is that a scene perfectly suited to each location, with actors dressed just right, is about to unfold…

Neville Stanikk, 2008

Bossington Hill from Horner Woods

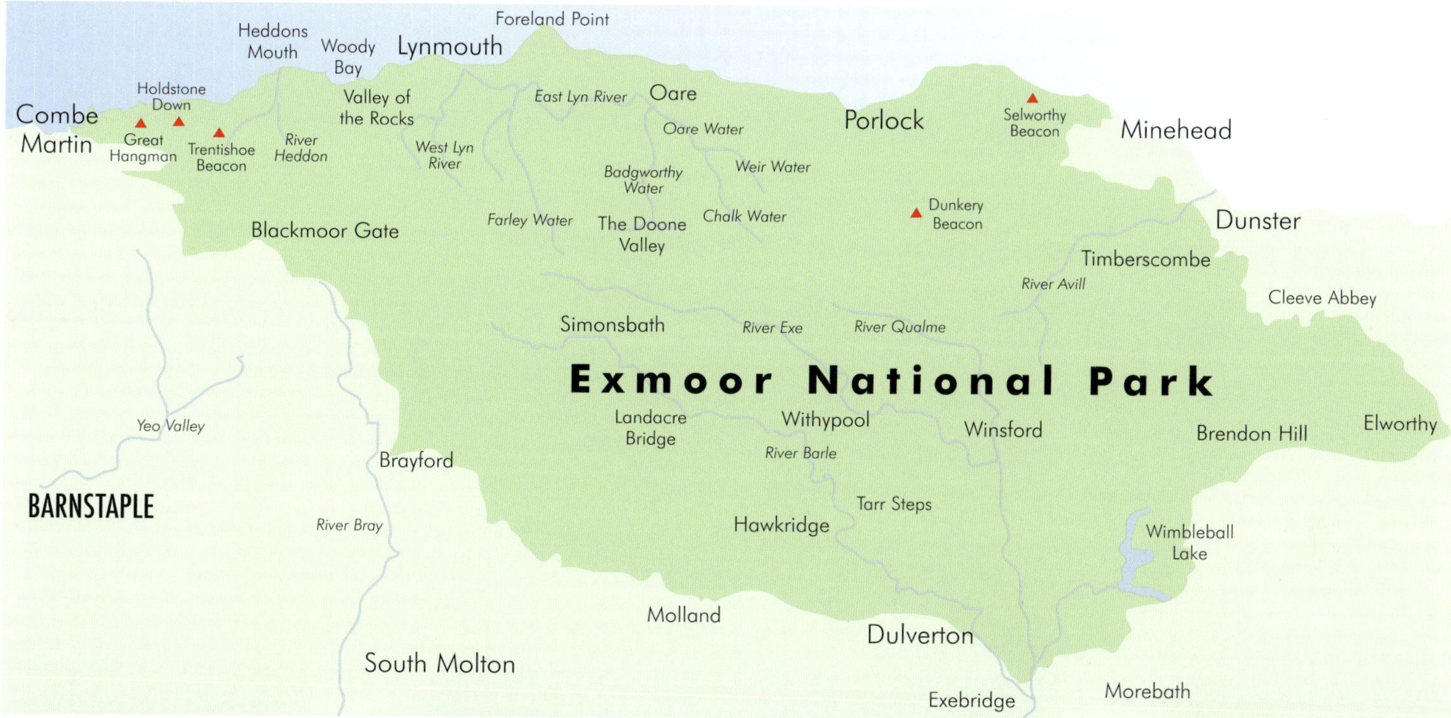

Exmoor National Park

Foreland Point

Heddons Mouth
Woody Bay
Lynmouth

Combe Martin

Holdstone Down

Valley of the Rocks

East Lyn River

Oare

Porlock

Minehead

Great Hangman
Trentishoe Beacon

River Heddon

West Lyn River

Oare Water

Selworthy Beacon

Badgworthy Water

Weir Water

Dunster

Blackmoor Gate

Farley Water

The Doone Valley

Chalk Water

Dunkery Beacon

Timberscombe

River Avill

Cleeve Abbey

Simonsbath

River Exe

River Qualme

Yeo Valley

Landacre Bridge

Withypool

Winsford

Brendon Hill

Elworthy

River Barle

Brayford

BARNSTAPLE

River Bray

Hawkridge

Tarr Steps

Wimbleball Lake

Molland

Dulverton

South Molton

Exebridge

Morebath

Combe Martin

Lee Abbey

Houses at Lynton

Heather and gorse at County Gate, with Southern Wood and the valley of the East Lyn River behind

Low tide on a hazy morning at Porlock Weir

Looking south east from Ley Hill
above Horner Woods

Early summer morning at Woody Bay, featuring one of the
many old lime kilns found along the Exmoor coast

Approaching summer storm
over Brendon Common

Waterfall on the East Lyn River at Watersmeet

Foreland Point from Lynmouth beach

Heather above Shillett Wood on Porlock Common

Shafts of sunset light fill the Brendon Valley from Holden Head on Countisbury Hill

The River Barle at Simonsbath
on a frosty morning

Looking west along the Exmoor
coast at Elwill Bay

The view south from a snowy Yenworthy Common

Weir Water at Robber's Bridge

Blizzard clouds above Porlock Allotment

Holly, hawthorn, heather and bracken on Porlock Common

A snow-covered Dunkery Beacon
from Luccott Cross

Storm over the Bristol Channel from the Valley of the Rocks, Lynton

Summer woodland near Cloutsham

Bossington Hill from Dunkery Beacon

The clapper bridge at Tarr Steps

'Snowdrop Valley' at North Hawkwell Wood below Wheddon Cross

Great Hangman and the Exmoor coast from Watermouth Cove

Badgworthy Water at Malmsmead

Bridge over the East Lyn River at Brendon and Leeford

Steps to the Town Hall at Dulverton
– uniquely free of cars!

Heather and a hawthorn tree at Porlock Allotment

The Rising Sun pub and cottages
on Mars Hill, Lynmouth

The River Barle at Sherdon Rock, looking towards Picked Stones

View towards Heale Down
from heather-covered slopes
of Trentishoe Beacon

No leaves yet. Early spring at Farley Water

Sheep in the snow on hills above Combe Martin

Farley Water with the slope
of Cheriton Ridge behind

Lamposts on Manor Green, Lynmouth
with the cliffs of Foreland Point behind

Heather and bracken cover Porlock Common with Bossington Hill in the distance

Still waters and frosty
morning at Simonsbath

The valley of Holcombe Water from Tom's Hill Barrows. Part of the 'Doone Valley'

Clapper bridge over the
River Barle at Tarr Steps

The Devil's Cheesewring and Mother Meldrum's Cave (although it's not much of a cave), Valley of the Rocks

The River Heddon and
Heddon's Mouth

Sea fog covers the entire Bristol Channel as seen by visitors on Porlock Hill

Badgworthy Water, otherwise known
as the Doone Valley

Dawn on Bossington Hill, looking towards Dunkery, with the edge of Allerford Plantation

High tide at Porlock Weir

Little Cornham Hill rises above early morning mist at Simonsbath

Sunrise through the mist at Halscombe Plantation, Simonsbath

Cascade in Lank Combe,
Badgworthy Water – the best candidate
for the 'waterslide' in *Lorna Doone*

Sunlit cobwebs at Simonsbath

South Regis Common, near Challacombe, in the snow

Yachts moored at Porlock Weir

Path through Badgworthy Woods in the 'Doone Valley'

A stream emerges on to the beach at Gore Point, Porlock Weir

Morning sunshine illuminates a copse of birch trees in
the Allerford Plantation on Bossington Hill

Conygar Tower, as seen through the morning haze from Bossington Hill

Cottages on Vicarage Street,
Minehead, with the parish church
of St Michael behind

Bossington Hill from the beach at Porlock Weir

Rocks along the spine
of Hurlestone Point

Waves lap the beach as North Hill rises above Minehead

Sunset at Porlock Weir with the
headland of Hurlestone Point
seen through masts

The very English landscape of Timberscombe Common

St Peter's church, Treborough

Frost left by freezing sea fog
on Dunkery Beacon

67

An autumn morning high tide at Minehead harbour

Cottages alongside the village green at Exford

St Mary's church at
Churchtown, Luxborough

Looking out to sea from Tivington Knowle

Autumn in the village of Horner

Horner Water, just before it seeps through the pebble ridge below Hurlestone Point

Wimbleball Lake, a reservoir in the southern part of Exmoor

Very still, clear waters
at Combe Martin

Bridge over the River Haddeo at Bury

Looking down on the the Exe valley at Helebridge

The cliffs of Countisbury Hill
tumble down to the sea with
Lynmouth and Hollerday Hill beyond

Autumn colours reflected in the River Exe at Hele Bridge

Boats in the harbour at Porlock Weir,
with the cottages of Turkey Island behind

These cows in the Bray valley arranged themselves very nicely for my photograph

The River Exe in shallows at
Larcombe Foot, west of Winsford

Dawn at Minehead with the 'spires' of Butlin's seen across the bay

The West Lyn River tumbles
over boulders at Barbrook

Looking down Thurley Combe on Wilmersham Common

View into Bagley Combe from Stoke Pero Common, with sea fog
covering Cloutsham and the slopes of Dunkery Beacon

Frost from freezing sea fog on Dunkery Beacon

Ice-coated trees on Culbone Hill

Looking west through a sunset haze at Brendon Common

Snowy winter twilight at Exe Head Bridge

Chetsford Water in the spring

Exmoor pony forages by a frosted tree on Porlock Hill

Ferns grow over the ruins of
Hollerday House at Lynton

Looking out from the Yarnmarket at Dunster

The High Street and Yarnmarket at Dunster

The River Barle at Cornham Brake
near Simonsbath

Path to the summit of Holdstone Down, one misty summer morning

The gnarled trunk of a hawthorn bush on Withypool Hill

Previous page
The rocky beach at Heddon's Mouth.
This and the valley behind being
a virtually unknown natural
wonder in my opinion

A very still River Barle at Simonsbath

Summer evening sunshine on Lester Cliff at Combe Martin

Clumps of windblown snow cling to a hedge on Castle Common

Almost like Africa or Borneo – looking down into Watersmeet fron Countisbury Hill

Stairs to the great hall at
Cleeve Abbey near Washford

The Royal Oak inn at Winsford

Hawthorn bush in bloom on Winsford Hill

Flagstoned path through Tarr Woods
with the River Barle alongside

Dawn on Winsford Hill

Ashton Cleave from County Gate, late on a snow-covered winter's day

Evening sunshine in
Burridge Woods, Dulverton

The Punchbowl from Winsford Hill on a very windy morning

Clump of Monkey Flowers on
the River Barle at
Cornham Brake near Simonsbath

A profusion of buttercups and red campions at Chibbet Post near Exford

Rocks and cliffs at Combe Martin.
Still water on a summer evening

Cold but clear morning at Withypool

Autumn leaves carpet the riverside path of the River Barle east of Withypool

Tufts of frosted grass on
Brendon Common

Shafts of sunlight illuminate Burridge Woods, near Dulverton

Trunks of wind-sculpted beech trees
on Yenworthy Common

Sunset storm light on cottages at Selworthy

The River Barle and bridge at Landacre

The inappropriately placed (at the entrance to a car park)
statue of Lorna Doone at Dulverton

A stream winds through the salt marshes at Porlock Weir

Larches in brilliant autumn colours above the Bray valley

Tables outside on
Bank Square, Dulverton

Rocks and cliffs at the base of Hurlestone Point

The River Bray flows out of
the village of Challacombe

Sunset haze turns the cliffs west of Porlock Weir into silhouettes

Low tide and early summer
morning at Combe Martin

A summer's day at Lynmouth harbour

A winter sunset from South Regis Common

Opposite page: A snowy River Barle seen from Cowcastle

A snow covered Yeo valley, just to the west of Exmoor

Moorland beech trees catch the winter light on Countisbury Hill

Looking towards Brayford from Bray Common

Fields covered in snow at sunset near Parracombe

Sheep graze on Countisbury Hill, with Foreland Point and the Bristol Channel in the background

Mist in the Bray valley from Leworthy,
seconds before dawn

The breakwater at Lynmouth harbour

Summer cumulo-nimbus clouds build up above Stoke Pero Common

Arlington Court, a National Trust property and home of the Chichester family, on the western side of Exmoor

Cottages on Church Steps, Minehead

Beech hedge against the sunset on Castle Common